Thinking in Different Colors

Jade Saenz

Presentation by *BookLeaf Publishing*

Web: www.bookleafpub.com

E-mail: info@bookleafpub.com

ISBN: 9789357446617

First edition 2022

Come Alive

Understand this
You are what you feel
Sometimes nothing seems real
We dream for escapes and wake just to break
You cannot come alive without finding yourself
This world was not made for the deceased
It is here for life
To show passion
The road is foggy and we must choose our path
wisely
Do not live to die
Come alive

You

Who are you?
Why do you do this to me?
I'm feeling déjà vu
But I don't know you
A glimpse of the past running through my mind
I cant help but feel lost in time
A glimpse of you and I have hope
But that's what hurts me most
I know you will never be real
It feels like sometimes things never heal
No matter who I see
I will never be set free
At least not from you

Unknown Love

I witness in a silent bliss your face
Every word you speak gives me a quick rush
It makes me weak wishing for a white noise
But instead I feel my face turn to blush
I feel the touch of your hand rush past me
I remember what it's like to feel whole
I'm in fear of everything we could be
You lifted a flame and awoke my soul
Gleaming with a bright passion within him
He leans in for a kiss no more fighting
No more need to hide in this room so dim
I now sit in this empty space writing
You gave me an unknown feeling of love
I now must have your body disposed of

The Sound of
Silence

Have you ever listened to the sound of silence?
Sit quietly and tell me what you hear
The sound of a million sunsets will ring in your
ear
Sensations like never before may occur
Rushing through your body
You may feel alone at first
Within seconds your mind will be lost
Free from your thoughts
The sound of silence will ring
And it will change everything
You will become a new being

Bullets in the Sky

She asked, "what are you so afraid of?"
"The crime, the blood?"
He answered, "the idea of love"
"Why?" She asked
"I've seen bullets fall from the sky." He
whispered very shy

Invisible

Do you remember me?
I live in your history
Worn out and old
But I never turned to stone
Can you hear me?
I scream all day and night
But you never hear a sound
Do you see me?
I'm always near
But I'm not your deepest fear
Please tell me there's something there
I can't live my life this bare
Someone find me sitting alone in this chair

The One That Got Away

We meet again
As more than friends
Every moment goes by in a flash
You're the one that got away
Not even one mistake
But it wasn't our fate
Every date ends in seconds
I miss you but you're so far away
Its only been a day
And again, you're the one that got away
But you've changed my life
Now I dream of you at night
But you're out of sight
Our last kiss goodnight
And you're back on your flight
The timings never right
I'll miss you once again
I know we're still friends
But I want to be with you until the very end

A Different Brain

There's so much noise
Even when it's quiet
I wish you could see it from my side
But I hide it
I have a million voices in my head
All with so much being said
Often times I just lay in bed
Because I can't face reality
It's like having two personalities
My emotions take over
I'm back on this roller coaster
I'm different from the others
They don't seem to suffer
I see the world a little different
The people around me can come off a little
ignorant
Sometimes I feel alone
It's like I'm in a different time zone
I'm very specific
When anything changes my day turns horrific
I wish it was easier to understand me
But my brain works different than those around
me

Faking it

She finally did the right thing
A moment of hurt
And it comes to the worst
She's stuck between the past and present
Looking at her arms
She thinks to herself
Almost a year and she can't take it
There's no more faking it
One sentence is spoken
She takes the blade
Not realizing the mistakes she's made
Regretting every pill she threw down the drain

Finding Yourself

In a contest with myself
I wonder whether to go North or South
My mind's an empty shelf
The words never come out
To find my happiness
In a world of disappointment
Ignorance is bliss
When is life's appointment?
The only way out is in
You must know yourself within

Screaming

I hear screams
But I'm happy in my dreams
I'm a ball of rage but seconds later its okay
Why do I scream?
I want you to be happy
I want to show you I care
Why do I only scare?
They run away from me
Its my fault but I can't control my thoughts
I'm trying to show you my love
But I never know what you're thinking of
I want to know you
I want you to get me
But in the end its a big mess and tragedy
There's feelings I can't control
And you don't feel the same
My feelings always remain
I just want to be sane
Until then I wait
But will it ever be enough?
I'm always in some kind of mental state

Forbidden Love

Everyday I'm suck
Because I know its forbidden love
When I'm in the water
I sink
I want you to take my hand
You're the only one who understands
Why can't we just have fun?
Instead I just run
Knowing I'll never reach the sun
Even when we feel the same
It's not allowed
It's almost insane
But even with that my heart remains
So I speak loud and proud

The Trains of the World

I hear the train
It calls my name
I don't understand why everyone is acting insane
I hide in my safe spot
In hopes no one sees me
I keep it locked
Please let me be
I'm hard to motivate
Because I can't always relate
I try to communicate
But I get ignored
I understand trains of the world
They sometimes stop
But they keep going
I'm a wiggle worm
At least thats what they tell me
And I don't always want people around me
Sometimes noises are too loud
But others calm me down
Occasionally I like to play
I play all day
I have a few friends

But I get overwhelmed and want to be alone
again
I'm on my own
But I know I'm not always alone

The Deep Blue

I see the ocean blue
It reminds me of you
All the waves
They're all the same
The current pulls me in
The rush of the wind on my skin
It calms me down
It's peaceful and quiet
My mind was a riot
Every day I'm in the deep blue
All the memories remain
The memories of you

The Game We Play

I don't get it
Why we must live in this world of grey?
Its something no one understands
We go from love to hate
And life becomes pain
But we still live through it
On and on we go
We bottle it up
Some tend to break
But in the end isn't it all the same?
A world of suffering
Yet we have so much faith
Never could tell why we sit here in the rain
Like leveling up in a game
But you run out of lives
And the pain stays
Until we start the next game
The one we call life

One More Day

So little time
So much to do
We still manage to make our way through
There's days we can't win
But we still hold that grin
There's no reason to hide
We still have pride
If we hold our head high
There's no time to waste
Just live life no matter the pace
Take it day by day
Because not everyone is here to stay

Lost in the Woods

I can't speak when there's people around me
I'm scared of what they think
I want to be noticed
But I don't know how
I'm just someone in the crowd
I try my best to blend in
But it seems it never works out in the end
They make it seem easy
But I've never understood
Why I always feel like I'm lost in the woods
I'll keep this up as long as I can
Hoping someone will find me
Maybe then I won't feel so alone
Because someone will finally set me free

A Moment of Peace

Busy as a bee
I just want to read
Just for an hour and nothing feels sour
Feel the cool freeze
A moment of peace
The smell of flowers
And the grass beneath me

Autism Acceptance

I ask a lot of questions
No one seems to get it
I've heard it all
I talk too much or I'm dull
I'm just trying to understand
Will you please give me a hand?
The world can be so cruel
Why are there so many hidden rules?
With a little more acceptance
Maybe we could end this
Take a moment and listen
Every chance your given
All we ask for is a chance
To prove that we're more than what you see at
first glance